T0019634

*to Rachel Machado
you're one in a melon*

INTRODUCTION

Puns are the best! Puns are the worst! Puns are even better when you share (and groan) with your friends and family! What makes puns so great and so awful at the same time? Well, they play on words, picking new words that sound like the ones you expect but aren't, or using words and phrases in ways that they weren't meant to be used. They're usually pretty clever, but not everyone appreciates the fine art of punning!

So why do we groan so much at something that's funny and even smart? Nobody really knows. We do know that puns go back a long way. Shakespeare used them all the time in his plays. By all accounts, his audiences loved whenever puns showed up, and even laughed out loud at them. Maybe our tastes have

changed over time. Maybe those people knew something we don't?

Anyway, just because puns are not always appreciat-
ed now doesn't mean that you shouldn't tell them. No!
In fact, it's even better that way! Flip though this book,
learn several good ones, and then go and tell them to
everyone. Better yet, take this book with you, find a
victim, and unleash one joke after another. Try to tell
at least five or six in a row . . . they'll be begging you to
stop. They might not laugh, but you will!

Be careful, though. If you spend too long reading
this, your time will be all *booked* up.

Enjoy this book, and the hundreds of punny jokes
inside!

WHAT KIND OF FISH HAS THE BIGGEST SHOES?

A clown fish!

What kind of candy bar is the funniest?

Snickers.

What kind of music does a mountain listen to?

Classic rock.

WHERE DOES A BIRD BORROW BOOKS?

At the flybrary.

~

WHY DO THE NUMBERS ONE TO TWELVE WORK THE HARDEST?

They're on the clock.

WHAT DID THE PIRATE BUY AFTER HE GOT HIS PATCH?

An eye-phone!

~

WHAT IS A SOUP'S FAVORITE SPORT?

Bowling.

WHAT KIND OF CAREER DID THE BOAT WANT TO BE IN?

Sails.

WHY CAN'T LAMPS BE TRUSTED?

They're too shady.

WHAT DOES A SHOWER DO ON NEW YEAR'S EVE?

Pops a bottle of shampoo.

Why do cakes smell so good?

They have a lot of flower.

....

What was the bath towel doing all day?

Just hanging out.

....

Where does Mozart bake his bread?

In the Beethoven.

———— //// ————

Why did the cookie
go to the doctor?

Because it was feeling crumby.

....

Why did the banana
go to the doctor?

Because it wasn't peeling well!

....

Why couldn't the walnut
shell get a job?

Because it was a nut case.

———— //// ————

WHAT DOES A GARDEN WEAR WITH ITS SHIRT?

A pair of plants!

➤

WHAT DO YOU CALL A COW WITHOUT LEGS?

Ground beef.

➤

WHEN DOES A DUCK WAKE UP?

At the quack of dawn!

WHY WON'T TEDDY BEARS EAT DESSERT?

They're always stuffed!

>>>———→

WHAT TYPE OF SANDALS DOES A FROG WEAR?

Open-toad.

>>>———→

WHAT'S A PIRATE'S FAVORITE LETTER?

RRRRRR.

Wanna hear a pizza joke?

Never mind, it's way too cheesy!

...

What did the syrup say to the waffle?

I love you a waffle lot!

...

What do you call the wife of a hippie?

A Mississippi!

Why are frogs so happy?

They eat whatever bugs them.

...

Why did the newlyweds buy stale baguettes?

They wanted to grow mold together!

...

Why are leopards bad at hide-and-seek?

They are always spotted!

WHAT'S THE BEST TIME TO GO TO THE DENTIST?

Tooth-hurty!

What do you call a classy sea creature?

Sofishticated!

What did the big flower say to the little flower?

Hey, bud!

WHAT DO YOU CALL A PIG WHO DOES KARATE?

Pork chop!

WHY DID THE TOMATO BLUSH?

It saw the salad dressing!

WHY ARE PASTRIES SO STUPID?

They donut know anything!

~

WHY COULDN'T THE PONY SING IN THE CHOIR?

He was a little horse!

WHY WAS THE BEE'S HAIR STICKY?

He used a honeycomb!

WHY ARE SKELETONS SO LONELY?

They have no body!

WHAT DO YOU CALL A SHOE MADE OUT OF A BANANA?

A slipper!

How do you organize a space party?

Planet!

....

What do you call a dog who has magic powers?

A Labracadabrador!

....

Why are daisies so supportive?

They be-leaf in you!

What do you call a bear with no teeth?

A gummy bear!

....

What do you call a Jedi from the Pacific Northwest?

Leak Skywater.

....

What did the famous eighteenth-century composer's chickens say?

Bach, Bach, Bach.

WHAT'S THE MOST MUSICAL PART OF A FISH?

The scales!

➤

WHAT DO YOU GET WHEN YOU CROSS SWEET POTATOES WITH A JAZZ BAND?

A yam session.

➤

WHAT HAPPENED AFTER THE BAKERY BURNED DOWN?

The business was toast.

WHAT DO YOU CALL AN AVOCADO WITH A MOHAWK HAIRCUT?

Punk guac.

≫——→

WHY COULDN'T THE BICYCLE STAY STANDING UP?

It was two tired.

≫——→

WHY CAN'T A HAND BE TWELVE INCHES LONG?

Because then it would be a foot.

Did you hear about the fire at the campground?

It was in tents.

...

Why are nesting dolls so inconsiderate?

Because they're full of themselves!

...

Did you hear about the butter rumor?

You probably shouldn't spread it.

Did you hear about the award-winning farmer?

He was outstanding in his field.

...

What's brown and sticky?

A stick!

...

Why was the new chimney in trouble?

It was too young to be smoking.

———— //// ————

DID YOU HEAR ABOUT THE PENCIL WITH TWO ERASERS?

It was pointless.

———— //// ————

Why was the sea being investigated?

Because it was a bit fishy.

What music do mummies like?

Wrap music.

WHAT DO YOU CALL A COW WITH ONLY TWO LEGS?

Lean beef.

~

WHAT DOES A VEGETARIAN ZOMBIE EAT?

Grains!

WHAT HAPPENED AFTER THE AUTHOR DIED?

She became a ghost writer.

~

WHY DID THE MAN DECIDE TO KEEP HIS BEARD?

It grew on him over time.

DID YOU HEAR THE HEAR THE BAD PAPER JOKE?

It was really tear-able!

WHY DO ACTORS SAY "BREAK A LEG" BEFORE A SHOW?

Because they're all part of the same cast.

WHERE DO RAVENS LIKE TO DRINK?

At the crowbar.

Why did the shoe go to heaven?

It had a good sole.

....

Why did the lobsters refuse to help?

Because they were shellfish!

....

What do you call a fish with no eyes?

A fsh!

Why are concert halls so cold?

Because they're usually full of fans.

....

What do you call a place where they make things that are just okay?

A satisfactory.

....

What do you give to a citrus fruit that needs help?

Lemon aid.

WHAT KINDS OF PHOTOS DO BOOKSHELVES TAKE?

Shelfies!

➤

WHAT DID THE HAMBURGER NAME ITS NEW BABY?

Patty!

➤

WHY DID THE MAN GET FIRED FROM A CALENDAR FACTORY?

He took a couple of days off.

WHY DIDN'T THE WOMAN GET HURT WHEN A SODA CAN HIT HER HEAD?

It was a soft drink.

≫——→

WHY DID THE SCIENTISTS PUT A KNOCKER ON THE FRONT DOOR?

To try to win the no-bell prize.

≫——→

WHY COULDN'T THE PHOTOGRAPHER TAKE A PICTURE OF THE FOG?

He mist his chance.

What did the eggs think of the joke?

It cracked them up.

...

How did the man feel after his lamp was stolen?

He was de-lighted.

...

Why was the lawyer so well dressed?

She had a good lawsuit.

How did the duck pay for her new lipstick?

She put it on her bill!

...

How do you make an egg roll?

Push it down the hill.

...

Why did the coffee report a crime?

It was mugged.

WHY ARE BAKERS SO GOOD AT MATH?

It's as easy as pi.

Did you read the new book about antigravity?

It's impossible to put down.

What do you call an ordinary potato that gives its opinion?

A common-tater.

WHAT DID THEY SAY TO THE GUY WHO INVENTED ZERO?

Thanks for nothing.

∾

DOES AN OCEAN OF ORANGE SODA EXIST?

No, it's just a Fanta-sea.

WHY SHOULDN'T YOU TRUST STAIRS?

Because they're always up to something.

WHAT HAPPENED WHEN THE BAKER ACCIDENTALLY SWALLOWED SOME FOOD COLORING?

She dyed a little inside.

WHY SHOULDN'T YOU BELIEVE AN ATOM?

Because they make up everything.

HOW DID THE ROMAN EMPEROR CUT HIS HAIR?

With a pair of Caesars.

WHY WERE MEDIEVAL TIMES CALLED THE DARK AGES?

Because there were so many knights.

Did you hear about the collection of candy canes?

They were all in mint condition.

....

What was the windmill's favorite kind of music?

It was a big metal fan.

....

Why did the teacher need glasses?

Her pupils were causing her problems.

What happens when you toss small ovens into the water?

You get microwaves.

....

Why didn't the woman want to go to a funeral at 10:00 a.m.?

She wasn't a mourning person.

....

What do you call a chicken's ghost?

A poultrygeist.

DID YOU HEAR THE BAD JOKE ABOUT THE GERMAN SAUSAGE?

It was the wurst!

>>>>———→

WHY COULDN'T THEY FIGURE OUT WHY THE COIN-MAKING MACHINE STOPPED WORKING?

It didn't make any cents.

>>>>———→

WHY DID THE MAN BUY A BOAT?

It was on sail.

WHY WAS THE PICTURE IN PRISON?

It was framed.

≫———→

WHAT HAPPENED WHEN THE PAST, PRESENT, AND FUTURE WALKED INTO A BAR?

It was tense.

≫———→

DID YOU HEAR ABOUT THE MAN WHO SUED THE AIRLINE FOR MISPLACING HIS LUGGAGE?

He lost his case.

How do spiders communicate?

With the world wide web!

...

What did the man who stole brake fluid say in his defense?

I can stop any time.

...

What does a pirate pay for corn on the cob?

A buccaneer!

What do you call a bee that can't decide?

A maybe!

...

What was the frog's new job at the hotel?

A bellhop.

...

What was the name of the owl magician?

Hoo-dini.

IF A T-REX HITS ITS HEAD, WHAT DOES IT GET?

Dino-sore!

Why was the train conductor fired?

He couldn't keep track of things.

Did you hear about the person who was accidentally buried alive?

It was a grave mistake.

WHY DID THE GARDENER WORK SLOWLY IN THE HERB GARDEN?

Because there was plenty of thyme.

～

WHAT DID MY MOM SAY WHEN SHE SAW HOW MESSY MY BOOK COLLECTION WAS?

You should be ashamed of yourshelf.

WHY DIDN'T THE POPPY SEEDS LEAVE THE CASINO?

They were on a roll.

~

HOW DOES A MOTORCYCLE LAUGH?

Yamahahahahaha.

WHAT DID THE BIRD SAY WHEN ITS FRIEND PRANKED IT?

Toucan play at that game!

WHY SHOULD YOU ALWAYS WASH A CHEESE SLICER AFTER USING IT?

It's for the grater good.

HOW DID THE TREE GET ONLINE?

It logged in.

Why should you never whisper secrets on a farm?

Because the corn has ears.

....

Why was winter not so good for Humpty Dumpty?

Because he'd already had a great fall.

....

What do you call a fake noodle?

An impasta.

Why wasn't the cat a good storyteller?

Because it only had one tail.

....

Why was VII so hard to catch?

Because it was a roamin' numeral.

....

What's the best way to keep your bagel from being stolen?

Put some lox on it.

WHY WAS THE DOG NAMED ROLEX?

He was a watchdog.

>>>—▶

WHAT DID THE MECHANIC SAY TO THE ANGRY JUMPER CABLE?

Don't start anything.

>>>—▶

WHAT HAPPENED WHEN THE GRAPE GOT STEPPED ON?

It let out a little wine.

DID YOU HEAR ABOUT THE GROUP OF RABBITS THAT JUMPED BACKWARDS?

They were a receding hare-line.

>>>——

WHY IS IT WARMER IN A CORNER?

Because it's ninety degrees.

>>>——

WHAT DID THE CAKE THINK OF THE WEDDING?

It was in tiers!

Why couldn't the coffee go out?

It was grounded!

...

Why did the banker quit her job?

She lost interest.

...

Why is waking up so amazing?

It's an eye-opening experience.

How did the rock climber set his tent up on the cliff?

He got the hang of it.

...

What is the elevator operator's job like?

It has its ups and downs.

...

How can you start a fire with a search engine?

Ask, and you'll get a lot of matches.

WHY DIDN'T THE FLUTE MADE FROM A MAPLE TREE WORK?

It wooden whistle.

What did the man say after eating a clock?

That was time-consuming!

Why did that man eat another clock?

He went back for seconds.

DID YOU HEAR ABOUT THE KIDNAPPING AT SCHOOL?

Don't worry, she woke up.

~

WHY DOESN'T THE SUN NEED TO GO TO COLLEGE?

It already has thousands of degrees.

WHY ARE CIRCLES SO USELESS?

Because they're pointless.

~

WHAT DO YOU CALL A BELT MADE OF WATCHES?

A waist of time.

WHERE DO DOGS GO WHEN THEY LOSE THEIR TAILS?

To a re-tail shop.

WHAT HAPPENED IN THE ART CONTEST?

It ended in a draw.

WHAT WOULD HAPPEN IF SNOWMEN ATTACKED?

You might get frost-bitten.

What do you call a nose that's all by itself?

Nobody knows . . .

....

Do you think this glass coffin will be successful?

Remains to be seen.

....

Why shouldn't you buy Velcro?

Because it's a rip-off.

What happened after the two antennas got married?

The reception was great!

....

Did you hear that neither of the gloves fit on her left hand?

It's all right now.

....

Did you hear the construction joke?

I'm still working on it.

WHY IS PETER PAN ALWAYS FLYING?

Because he Neverlands!

>>>>--->

DID YOU HEAR ABOUT THE AMAZING NEW SHOVEL?

It's ground-breaking!

>>>>--->

WHAT DO YOU CALL A FAMOUS OCEAN ANIMAL?

A starfish.

HOW DID THE POLICE FIND THE ROADWORKER WHO WAS STEALING THINGS?

When they searched his place, all the signs were there.

>>>——>

WHAT'S THE BEST MUSICAL INSTRUMENT?

Well, accordion to a new survey . . .

>>>——>

WHY DID THE MAN QUIT HIS NEW JOB AS A PENCIL SHARPENER AFTER HIS FIRST DAY?

He just didn't get the point.

Why did one banana like the other?

It was a-peeling!

...

Why would you give away old batteries?

Because they're free of charge!

...

How do spies keep warm?

They go undercover.

Why can't Cinderella play soccer?

She always runs away from the ball.

...

What did one magnet say to the other?

You're really attractive!

...

How did the hipster burn her mouth?

She ate her food before it was cool.

———— //// ————

DID YOU HEAR ABOUT THE NEW BAND, 999 MEGABYTES?

They still haven't gotten a gig.

———— //// ————

What did the man who inhaled helium think?

He spoke highly of it.

~

How does one sea greet another?

They wave.

DID YOU HEAR ABOUT THE JOB THE CARPENTER DID?

She nailed it!

WHY DID THE GHOST WANT ALCOHOL?

Because it liked boos.

WHAT DO YOU CALL TWO OCTOPUSES THAT LOOK EXACTLY ALIKE?

Itentacle.

~

WHY DID THE TREE WANT MORE FRIENDS?

It wanted to branch out.

WHY WOULDN'T THE SKELETON ASK ANOTHER SKELETON OUT ON A DATE?

It didn't have the guts to do it.

WHAT DO YOU CALL AN ALLIGATOR WITH A GPS?

A navigator.

WHAT DID THE KID GET WHO WAS LATE FOR PORK DINNER?

The cold shoulder.

Why did the choir stop singing the Hallelujah Chorus?

They just couldn't Handel it!

....

What did one rope say to the other when asked if it could help?

"I'm a frayed knot."

....

What happened when the rainbow took a test?

It passed with flying colors.

Why was the fish sent to jail?

Because it was gill-ty.

....

What did the football coach say to the store clerk?

I want a quarter back.

....

What's one thing rock climbers should never do?

Take their work for granite.

WHAT DO YOU GET WHEN A PIANO FALLS DOWN A MINE SHAFT?

A-flat miner.

>>>———>

WHAT'S THE BEST THING ABOUT A WHITEBOARD?

It's re-markable!

>>>———>

DID YOU HEAR THE BONE JOKE?

It's quite humerus.

WHAT DID THE BUFFALO SAY WHEN HIS BOY WENT AWAY FOR THE WEEKEND?

Bison.

>>>→

HAVE YOU TRIED THIS CORN PUDDING?

It's a-maize-ing!

>>>→

WHAT DID ANCIENT EGYPTIANS EAT AS FAST FOOD?

King Tutty-fried chicken.

Why does it hurt to touch a window?

Because you can feel the pane.

...

How does a basketball player eat a cookie with milk?

By dunking it!

...

What happened when the tomato fell behind?

It had to ketchup!

Why did police think the artist had committed the crime?

Because he was a bit sketchy.

...

What does a joke teller eat for breakfast?

Pun-cakes.

...

Did you hear about the mugger who attacked people in an elevator?

It was wrong on so many levels.

WHAT DID ONE GLACIER SAY TO THE OTHER?

Ice to meet you!

What did one hat say to the other?

I'll go on a head.

Why did the woman run around her bed?

To catch up on her sleep.

WHAT HAPPENED WHEN SOMEONE SENT TEN PUNS TO THEIR FRIEND TO MAKE THEM LAUGH?

No pun in ten did.

~

WHY DO COWS WEAR COWBELLS?

Because their horns don't work!

DID YOU HEAR THE NEWS ABOUT ICE CREAM?

No, give me the scoop!

―✑―

WHAT ABOUT THE COW WHO WAS SURE SHE'D EXPERIENCED SOMETHING BEFORE?

It was deja-MOO.

WHY WAS THE CAT KICKED OUT OF THE CARD GAME?

He was a cheetah!

WHY DID THE GHOSTS LIKE HAUNTING AN ELEVATOR?

It lifted their spirits!

WHAT'S A SKELETON'S FAVORITE MUSICAL INSTRUMENT?

The trom-bone.

Why did the
ocean cry?

Because it was blue.

....

What do you call a
sleeping male cow?

A bull-dozer.

....

Why was the pig
called "Ink"?

*Because he kept running
out of the pen.*

What do you call a cute entryway?

A-door-able.

....

What is an atomic scientist's favorite food?

Fission chips.

....

Did you hear they're finally making a TV show about clocks?

It's about time.

WHAT DID ONE SHOE SAY TO THE OTHER?

I'm a bit tied up at the moment.

>>>———➤

WHERE DOES A SNOWMAN KEEP ITS MONEY?

In a snow bank.

>>>———➤

WHICH ANIMAL LIKES TO PLAY BASEBALL?

A bat.

HOW DID THE BIRD LEARN TO FLY?

It just winged it.

≫——→

HAVE YOU SEEN THOSE NEW CORDUROY PILLOWCASES?

They're making headlines.

≫——→

WHY DID THE GYM CLOSE DOWN?

It wasn't working out.

What do you call a rodent who wants to stay secret?

Anony-mouse.

...

Did you hear about the man who was afraid of the wall outside his house?

He got over it.

...

Did you hear about the short fortune-teller who escaped from jail?

It was a small medium at large.

What happened to the two people who each stole half of a calendar?

They both got six months.

...

Did you hear that noisy tennis game?

It was quite a racquet!

...

Where do cows go on dates?

The MOO-vies.

WHAT HAPPENED TO THE WOMAN WHO WANTED A BRAIN TRANSPLANT?

She changed her mind.

What's a horse's favorite kind of story?

A pony tale!

~

What did the man say to the buzzing fly?

Stop bugging me!

WHAT DO YOU CALL A GROUP OF FUNNY COWS?

A laughing stock.

WHAT WAS THE KING'S FAVORITE KIND OF WEATHER?

Reign.

WHAT DO YOU SAY TO A GHOST WHO'S REALLY TRYING TO DO THEIR BEST?

That's the spirit!

~

WHY WAS MONEY FALLING FROM THE SKY?

There was a change in the weather.

CAN YOU HELP ME LOOK FOR MY LOST CLOCK?

I don't have the time.

WHAT HAPPENS AFTER MUSICIANS DIE?

They de-compose.

WHY WAS THE AUSTRALIAN ANIMAL HIRED?

It had great koala-fications.

Why did the donut shop close?

The owner was tired of the hole business.

....

What did the waiter say to the skeleton?

Bone-appétit!

....

How do they measure things on farms?

In barn yards.

What do you call someone who's afraid of Santa?

Claus-trophobic!

....

What do you call a rose talking on the phone?

A call-i-flower.

....

What happened when you went to the seafood gym?

You pulled a mussel.

HAVE YOU HEARD THE JOKE ABOUT THE PEACH?

It's pit-iful.

>>>————➤

WHAT'S THE ONE PLACE IN A HOUSE A ZOMBIE WON'T GO?

The living room.

>>>————➤

WHAT DID THE COMPUTER SAY AFTER TAKING A LONG TRIP?

That was a hard drive!

WHERE DO AUTOMOBILES LIKE TO HAVE FUN?

At the car-nival.

WHAT WAS THE NAME OF THE ROBOT WHO HAD TO TAKE A DIFFERENT ROUTE?

R2-Detour.

WHAT DID THE BEACH SAY WHEN THE TIDE CAME IN?

Long time, no sea.

What kind of candy do planets like?

Mars bars.

...

What kind of music do planets like?

Nep-tunes.

...

Why don't towels like goofy jokes?

Because they have a dry sense of humor.

Why should you trust a calculator?

Because you can count on it.

...

What happened to the frog who parked illegally?

It got toad.

...

How did the bird of prey feel when it lost what it was hunting?

Hawkward!

WHY DID
THE DRIED
FRUIT NOT
AGREE WITH
THE REST
OF THE
PANTRY?

It had its raisins.

What did the dolphin say when it bumped into a whale?

Sorry, it wasn't on porpoise!

Why is Ireland's capital the fastest growing?

It's Dublin every day.

DID YOU HEAR THE OWL'S NEW JOKE?

It was a hoot!

~

WHAT SPORTS CAR DOES A CAT DRIVE?

A Fur-rari.

HOW DO YOU CALM DOWN A CRYING BABY ALIEN?

You rocket to sleep.

~

WHAT KIND OF CLOTHES DO STORM CLOUDS HAVE?

Thunderwear.

WHAT DID ONE BLADE OF GRASS SAY TO THE OTHER WHEN THERE WAS NO RAIN?

We'll just have to make dew.

DID YOU HEAR ABOUT THE EXPENSIVE WIG?

It was too high a price toupee!

WHAT DO YOU CALL A SHIP ON THE OCEAN FLOOR THAT'S VERY WORRIED?

A nervous wreck.

119

What happens if you bother someone while they're working on a puzzle?

You hear some crosswords.

....

Did you hear about the funny sea monster?

He's Kraken me up!

....

What do you call an alligator who's a thief?

A crookadile.

How come you are friends with only twenty-five letters of the alphabet?

I don't know Y.

....

Why did the man get fired from the bank?

When a customer asked him to check her balance, he pushed her over.

....

Why is an orchestra a dangerous place?

It has a lot of violins.

WHAT HAPPENED TO THE HOUSE WHOSE TOILET WAS STOLEN?

Police had nothing to go on.

>>—→

WHAT DID THE MAN SAY WHEN HE WALKED INTO A BAR?

Ow!

>>—→

WHAT KIND OF DRINK CAN BE HARD TO SWALLOW?

Reali-tea.

WHY DID THE FAMILY SELL THEIR VACUUM?

It was just collecting dust.

>>>⟶

WHAT'S A COW'S FAVORITE HOLIDAY?

Moo Year's Eve.

>>>⟶

WHAT DO YOU GET WHEN YOU CROSS A CAT WITH FATHER CHRISTMAS?

Santa Claws.

How do you defend a castle made out of cheese?

With Moat-zarella.

...

What happened to the origami business?

It folded.

...

What's a cat's favorite color?

Purrrple!

Why couldn't the chef decide to serve pancakes for breakfast?

She kept on waffling.

...

What's the definition of a vaccination?

A jab well done.

...

Did you hear the song about a tortilla?

It's wrap music.

WHY DID THE PLUM ASK THE CHERRY TO DINNER?

It couldn't find a date.

How much space should you plan for growing fungi?

As mushroom as possible!

What did the chef say as the water boiled away?

You will be mist.

WHY DID THE MAN ACCIDENTALLY CALL THE HOLE IN THE GROUND A SEWER?

He meant well.

WHAT KIND OF MUSIC ARE BALLOONS AFRAID OF?

Pop music.

WHY WAS THE MATH BOOK SAD?

Because it had so many problems.

***

DID YOU SEE THE AD FOR BURIAL PLOTS?

That's the last thing I need!

WHY WAS THE PHILOSOPHER SO BUSY?

Because he had a lot on his Plato.

WHAT KIND OF MUSIC IS POPULAR ON GOLF COURSES?

Swing.

WHAT DO YOU GET FROM A COW THAT'S BEEN PAMPERED?

Spoiled milk.

What did one needle say to the other?

You're looking sharp.

....

What did the two cats do after arguing?

Hiss and make up.

....

What's a tropical bird's favorite movie?

The Parrots of the Caribbean.

Why did the girl bring a ladder to class?

She wanted to get into high school.

....

Why did the egg comedian fail?

All it had were bad yolks.

....

What did the man who walked into a bar with a piece of concrete say?

I'll have a drink, and one for the road.

WHY WAS THE BARBER DISQUALIFIED FROM THE HAIR-TRIMMING COMPETITION?

He didn't make the cut.

>>>———>

WHAT DID THE POLICE OFFICER SAY TO HER STOMACH?

You're under a vest!

>>>———>

WHY DOES THE WOMAN KEEP HER OLD CLOTHING?

Because it really suits her.

WHY DID REARRANGING ITS FURNITURE HELP THE RESTAURANT?

Because now, the tables have turned.

>>>———→

WHAT DO YOU CALL A TRAIN THAT LIKES GUM?

A chew chew.

>>>———→

WHEN IS A DOOR NOT A DOOR?

When it's ajar.

Did you hear about the rowboat sale?

It's an oar-deal!

...

Why didn't the skeleton go to the party?

Because it had nobody to go with.

...

Do you know a good elevator joke?

Sorry, I can't come up with one.

If we breathe oxygen in the day, what do we breathe at night?

Night-trogen!

...

What do you call a pen without a top?

De-cap-itated.

...

What happened when the students tied all their shoes together?

They took a class trip.

WHAT'S A PIRATE'S OTHER FAVORITE KEY ON A KEYBOARD?

The C.

Which of King Arthur's knights was shaped like a circle?

Sir Cumference.

Why do seagulls fly over the sea?

If they flew over the bay, they'd be bagels!

WHAT DO YOU CALL A HARE WHO TELLS BAD JOKES?

A punny rabbit.

~

WHY WAS SIX STILL HUNGRY?

Because seven ate nine.

WHAT DID THE DENTIST SAY ON THE WOMAN'S FOURTH VISIT?

You know the drill.

~

WHAT'S ANOTHER NAME FOR A TOASTER?

A tanning bread.

HAVE YOU BEEN TO THE FUNNY MOUNTAIN?

It's hill-arious!

HOW DO YOU SPOIL YOUR APPETITE?

It's a piece of cake!

HAVE YOU HEARD ABOUT THE PRISON LIBRARY?

It has its prose and cons.

Which animal doesn't tell the truth?

A lion.

....

Did you hear the joke about the omelette?

It was eggcellent!

....

Why can't the ocean lie very well?

Because people sea right through it.

What did the photon say at the hotel check-in desk?

No luggage, I'm traveling light.

....

Do you know sign language?

Yes, it's really handy!

....

Did you hear about the mean dentist?

He hurts your fillings.

DID YOU SEE THE THEATER SHOW ABOUT PUNS?

It was a play on words.

WHY IS SWITZERLAND SO GREAT?

Well, its flag is a big plus.

DID YOU HEAR ABOUT THE TREE WHEN SPRING CAME?

It was re-leaved.

WHY DID THE LAWYER HAVE MEXICAN FOOD FOR LUNCH?

To get some case-ideas.

≫——→

DID YOU HEAR ABOUT THE CHILD WHO WOULDN'T TAKE A NAP?

She was resisting a rest.

≫——→

DO YOU LIKE USING A STRAW?

No, those are for suckers.

What language does a bridge speak?

Span-ish.

...

What do you call a dinosaur that knows a lot of words?

A thesaurus.

...

What side dish did the rulers of Russia like the most?

Czar-dines.

What happens if you don't pay the exorcist his fee?

You get repossessed.

...

What happened to the man who made fake money?

He was arrested at his apart-mint.

...

What do you call a goose in a tuxedo who tells lies?

A propa-ganda.

WHAT HAPPENED WHEN DAVID HAD HIS ID STOLEN?

We had to call him Dav.

What do you call a horse
who disagrees with you?

A neigh-sayer!

What did the conductor
say when she found her
missing sheet music?

Score!

HOW DO YOU STOP A BULL FROM CHARGING?

Take away its credit card.

WHERE DID THE GENERAL KEEP HIS ARMIES?

In his sleevies.

WHY WAS THE NORSE GOD BANNED FROM PLAYING GAMES?

He was a Thor loser.

~

WHAT DID THE PIRATE SAY ON HIS EIGHTIETH BIRTHDAY?

Aye, matey!

WHAT HAPPENED TO THE MAN WHO TURNED INVISIBLE AND WANTED TO SEE A DOCTOR?

No one could see him for weeks.

WHAT ABOUT THE MAN WHO SWALLOWED SEVERAL SMALL, PLASTIC HORSES?

The doctor said his condition was stable.

DID YOU KNOW THAT SOMEONE HAS BEEN ADDING DIRT TO MY GARDEN?

The plot thickens!

Why didn't one boat want to go along with what the others were doing?

It was pier pressure.

....

Why is your nose in the middle of your face?

It's the scenter of attention.

....

Can I be frank?

No, your name's Jim.

Why do teenagers get together in odd numbers?

Because they can't even.

....

What do you call too many dogs?

A roverdose.

....

Is it easy for you to sleep?

Yes, I could do it with my eyes closed!

WHAT HAPPENED WHEN THE REPAIRMAN COULDN'T FIX THE WASHING MACHINE?

He threw in the towel.

➤➤➤

WHY DID THE THIEF GO INTO THE BATHROOM?

They wanted to take a shower.

➤➤➤

WHY DID THE GRAVEYARD HAVE A FENCE?

Because people were dying to get in.

WHY DID THE SCULPTOR PUT HER HANDS IN THE NEW CLAY?

She wanted to make a good first impression.

>>>———

DID YOU HEAR ABOUT THE JOKE THAT WAS ALWAYS ON TIME?

It was very pun-ctual.

>>>———

WHY DO YOU LIKE TAKING SELFIES?

I always pictured myself doing it.

Why should you never talk about infinity with a math teacher?

Because they'll go on about it forever.

...

What happened to your submarine business?

It took a dive.

...

Isn't your daughter still a baby?

She grew out of it.

Can February March?

No, but April May.

...

Have you heard the other joke about Peter Pan?

It never gets old.

...

What did the farmer say to the sheep that was hiding?

I see ewe!

DID YOU HEAR ABOUT THE NEW BROOM?

It's sweeping the nation!

Why did the woman using an umbrella look sick?

Because she was under the weather.

What is that necktie doing?

Just hanging around.

DID YOU HEAR THE STORY ABOUT THE HAUNTED REFRIGERATOR?

It's chilling!

~

WHY WAS THE STEREO INVITED TO THE CONFERENCE?

It was the guest speaker.

DO YOU KNOW THE WOMAN FROM THE VEGETARIAN CLUB?

No, I've never met herbivore.

~

WHAT DOES A MULE USE TO GET OPEN A LOCKED DOOR?

A don-key.

WHY DIDN'T YOU LEARN TO DRIVE A STICK SHIFT?

I couldn't find a manual.

WHY WAS THE BULLET OUT OF WORK?

It got fired.

WHAT KIND OF BREAD DO YOU WEAR ON YOUR FEET?

Loafers.

What kind of climbing device is remarried?

A step-ladder.

....

Have you heard about those new reversible jackets?

I can't wait to see how they turn out!

....

What happens if you leave cookies in the oven for too long?

You burn calories.

What happened when two silkworms raced each other?

It ended in a tie.

....

What did the ghost teacher say to its ghost students?

Let me walk you through this again.

....

Did you understand when I explained the word "many" to you?

Yes, thanks, it means a lot.

DID YOU HEAR ABOUT THE KIDS WHO DRESSED UP AS ALMONDS FOR HALLOWEEN?

Everyone thought they were nuts.

➤➤➤

WHY WERE YOU FIRED FROM YOUR JOB AT THE ORANGE JUICE FACTORY?

I couldn't concentrate.

➤➤➤

HAVE YOU HEARD THE NEW VEGETABLE JOKE?

It's really corny.

WHAT HAPPENED WHEN THE ACTOR CHEWED HIS PENCIL WHILE READING HAMLET?

Now you can't tell if it's 2B or not 2B.

>>>——→

WHY DO YOU ENJOY SOCCER?

It's just for kicks!

>>>——→

DID YOU HEAR ABOUT THE REALLY BAD ELECTRICIAN?

People were shocked when they found out.

What did the man think when he got a new universal remote control?

This changes everything!

...

Did you forget how to throw a boomerang?

Don't worry, it'll come back to you.

...

Do you have a bookmark?

My name is Steve.

Do you understand the sea's philosophy?

It's really deep.

...

Why was the woman fired from the candle factory?

She wouldn't work wick-ends.

...

Why was the concert played only on piano bass notes?

It was a low-key affair.

HOW DO PRISONERS CALL EACH OTHER?

On cell phones.

What's the loudest pet you can have?

A trumpet.

What did the bartender say to the sandwich?

We don't serve food here.

WHAT DID THE WOMAN WHO WAS AFRAID OF ELEVATORS DO?

She took steps to avoid them.

❧

WHY DID THE GHOST CROSS THE ROAD?

To get to the Other Side.

WHAT DID THE YOUNG SAILOR GET ON HIS REPORT CARD?

Seven Cs.

~

HOW MANY INSECTS DO YOU NEED TO RENT AN APARTMENT?

Tenants.

WHAT DID THE POLICE DO TO THE CHEESE SANDWICH THEY ARRESTED?

They grilled it.

WHAT DO YOU CALL TOO MANY ALIENS?

Extraterrestrials.

WHY DID THE INVISIBLE MAN TURN DOWN THE JOB?

He just couldn't see himself doing it.

What do you call a broken can opener?

A can't opener!

....

Why haven't we heard the joke about the bed?

Because it hasn't been made up yet.

....

Did you hear about the restaurant on the moon?

Good food, but no atmosphere.

————— //// —————

What did the drummer name his twins?

Anna One, Anna Two.

....

Why did the woman buy a sale TV with the volume button stuck?

Because she couldn't turn it down.

....

When does a joke become a dad joke?

When it's apparent.

————— //// —————

DID YOU HEAR THE JOKE ABOUT UNEMPLOYMENT?

It doesn't work.

>>>——►

WHAT HAPPENED TO THE CHILD WITH PHOTOGRAPHIC MEMORY?

He never really developed it.

>>>——►

HOW WAS THE HEAVY METAL CONCERT?

It was ironic.

WHAT DO YOU CALL A MEAN THIEF GOING DOWNSTAIRS?

A condescending con descending.

>>>——→

WHY DID THE ASTRONAUT WANT TO BE ALONE?

She needed her space.

>>>——→

WHAT DID THE OCEAN SAY WHEN IT HEARD A BAD PUN?

I sea what you did there.

How does a con man sleep?

He lies on one side, and then lies on the other.

...

What are the strongest days of the week?

Saturday and Sunday; the rest are weekdays.

...

Why didn't the farmer want a well?

She'd have to dig deep to afford it.

What do you call a vampire duck?

Count Quack-ula.

...

What do you do if you're Hungary?

Czech the menu.

...

How was the Turkey?

It had a bit too much Greece.

DID YOU AT LEAST FINNISH YOUR FOOD?

*Yes, but there was Norway
I could eat any more.*

Why did the doctor send everyone home?

Because she lost her patients.

Which dinosaur likes hip-hop?

The veloci-rap-tor.

WHY ARE HOUSES WITH BASEMENTS MORE POPULAR?

Because they're best cellars.

WHERE DO YOU PUT A CHRISTMAS TREE?

Between a Christmas two and a Christmas four.

DID YOU HEAR ABOUT THE MUSHROOM THAT WAS GREAT TO HANG OUT WITH?

It was a real fungi.

~

WHY DID THE RABBIT LIKE THE DIAMOND?

Because it was twenty-four carats.

WHAT DOES THE SMALL BODY OF WATER DO WHEN IT'S ALONE?

It pond-ers life.

WHY DO GOLFERS BRING A SPARE PAIR OF PANTS?

In case they get a hole in one.

WHAT DO YOU CALL SMALL PIECES OF CLOTH YOU CAN SLEEP ON?

Napkins.

—— //// ——

Do you need to go to a tailor?

Sew it seams.

....

What did one earthquake say to the other?

It's not my fault!

....

Why should you be quiet near your medicine cabinet?

Because of the sleeping pills.

—— //// ——

How much does Santa's sleigh cost?

Nothing, it's on the house.

....

What do you call two birds stuck together?

Velcrows.

....

What happened to the man with two kidneys?

He grew up, and now they're adult knees.

DID YOU KNOW SOMEONE STOLE MY DICTIONARY?

I have no words for my anger.

>>>———>

WHAT KIND OF TREE CAN YOU WIPE YOUR HANDS ON?

A palm tree.

>>>———>

WHAT DO YOU CALL THE CHANGE IN YOUR POCKETS THAT GOES THROUGH THE WASHING MACHINE?

Laundered money.

DID YOU HEAR ABOUT THE HOUSE THAT WAS PAINTED WHITE?

It paled in comparison to the previous color.

≫⟶

WHY COULDN'T THE VENTRILOQUIST DO LAST NIGHT'S SHOW?

She threw out her voice.

≫⟶

HAVE YOU HEARD THE BALLOON JOKE?

It's a bit long-winded.

Why did the two fonts get divorced?

They just weren't each other's type.

...

Where do you buy chicken broth?

At the stock market.

...

Why can't Elsa hold a balloon?

She would let it go.

Why did the octopus beat the shark in a fight?

Because it was well-armed.

...

What do cows tell their children at bedtime?

Dairy tales.

...

What do you call a small soft drink without an apple in it?

A mini apple-less mini soda.

WHY DON'T VAMPIRES GO TO BARBECUES?

They're afraid of the steak.

———— //// ————

If you learn enough
of these jokes,
what will you be?

Pun-stoppable!

~

If the Marines can't
do the job, who
do you send in?

The sub-Marines.

———— //// ————

WHAT DID THE DOG SAY WHEN IT SAT DOWN ON SANDPAPER?

Ruff!

~

DID YOU HEAR ABOUT THE PROPRIETOR OF THE SHOE SHOP?

He's the sole owner.

WHAT DID THE CUSTOMER SAY TO THE BANKER WHO WOULDN'T STOP BOTHERING HER?

Leave me a loan!

~

DID YOU KNOW THAT MY FRIEND BROKE HER THUMB YESTERDAY?

On the other hand, she's fine!

WHAT WILL GOING TO BED WITH MUSIC ON GIVE YOU?

A sound sleep.

WHY IS THE TRACTOR SO DIFFERENT NOW?

Because it turned into a field.

WHAT KIND OF SHOES DO NINJAS WEAR?

Sneakers.

Why would you only buy nine racquets?

Because tennis too many.

....

What do you call cowboy clothes?

Ranch dressing!

....

What happened to the bomb that didn't go off the first time?

It refused.

Where do mummies go to get their bones worked on?

The Cairo-practor.

....

Why don't cannibals eat clowns?

Because they taste funny.

....

Did you hear the pig joke?

It was boar-ing.

WHERE CAN YOU IMPRISON A SKELETON?

In a rib cage.

➤➤➤

WHY DID THE WOMAN QUIT HER JOB AT THE HAIRDRESSER'S?

She wasn't cut out for it.

WHAT'S THE PROBLEM WITH LONG FANTASY STORIES?

They tend to dragon.

>>>———

DO YOU HAVE TALL FRIENDS THAT YOU ADMIRE?

Yes, I really look up to them.

>>>———

DID YOU HEAR ABOUT THE HUMAN CANNONBALL?

He got fired.

How do lumberjacks access their computers?

They log on.

...

Where do people who tell too many bad jokes end up?

In the pun-itentiary.

...

What did Nick say when his friend asked for five cents?

That he was Nicholas.

How is Saturn like a circus?

It has three rings.

...

Who walked into a bar?

A careless gymnast.

...

What happened when the clock accidentally went off at **4:00** a.m.?

It was alarming.

WHICH BARBARIAN ATTACKED ROME WITH BAD JOKES?

Attila the Pun!

How do you fix a train that can't hear so well?

With an engine-ear.

~

How did the dog stop the movie?

With the paws button!

DID YOU HEAR ABOUT THE BRICK COMPANY'S TRUCK THAT CRASHED?

It was just a few blocks down the road.

WHAT DO YOU GET IF YOU PUT A RADIO IN THE REFRIGERATOR?

Cool music.

WHAT KIND OF CHEESE ISN'T YOURS?

Nacho cheese!

HOW DID THE VIOLINIST GET AN ORCHESTRA AUDITION?

She asked a friend to pull some strings.

WHAT DO YOU CALL A PEA THAT FALLS OFF THE PLATE?

An escapee!

WHY DID THE MAN WANT THE SAUNA ALL TO HIMSELF?

He has selfish steam issues.

WHY DID THE GARDENER BUY SO MUCH SOIL AT A DISCOUNT?

It was dirt cheap!

Why was the half-man, half-horse always bragging?

He had to be the centaur of attention!

....

Why did the chicken cross the playground?

To get to the other slide.

....

Did you hear that scientists have made an artificial allergy?

They made it from scratch.

Have you heard the garbage joke?

Actually, it's rubbish.

....

How do you know the horse is sad?

It has a long face.

....

What is the kindest dinosaur?

A plesiosaur!

WHY WAS THE TRACK AND FIELD STAR LATE TO THE MEET?

She ran out of time.

>>>→

HOW DO YOU MAKE A SQUID LAUGH?

Tentacles.

>>>→

WHY ISN'T THE GROUP OF COWS FAMOUS?

Because no one has herd of them.

HAVE YOU SEEN THE CHILD WHO SKIPS ROPE AND READS AT THE SAME TIME?

She always jumps to conclusions.

>>>——►

WHAT'S A SQUIRREL'S FAVORITE SODA?

Oak-a-cola.

>>>——►

WHAT DID ONE SHEEP SAY TO ANOTHER AS SHE WAS LEAVING?

I wool see you later.

What do you call the answer to a bad joke?

A pun-ch line!

...

What do baseball players eat on?

Home plates.

...

What do you call a knight who's too scared to joust?

Sir Render.

What do you call a chicken crossing the road?

Poultry in motion.

...

What did the cat who didn't believe the other cat say?

You've got to be kitten me!

...

What do you get when you cross a dinosaur with a pig?

Jurassic pork.

My teacher said,
"Name two pronouns."

I said, "Who, me?"

~

I can turn into a cat.

Don't ask meow.